MARITIME
SEAFOOD
Chowders, Soups and More

MARITIME SEAFOOD

Chowders, Soups and More

by Chef Paul Lucas

The Acorn Press
Charlottetown
2013

ACORNPRESS

P.O. Box 22024
Charlottetown, Prince Edward Island
C1A 9J2
acornpresscanada.com

Printed in China
Design by Matt Reid
Editing by Laurie Brinklow
Cover photography and author photo by Mike Needham
Interior food photography (pages ii, 36, 48, 62, 81, 85, 88) by Mike Needham
Landscape photography and lobster (page 60) by Melissa Buote
Other photographs by Paul Lucas

Library and Archives Canada Cataloguing in Publication

Lucas, Paul, 1968-
        Maritime seafood chowders, soups and more / Paul Lucas.

Includes index.
ISBN 978-1-894838-94-8

                1. Cooking (Seafood). 2. Soups--Maritime Provinces.
3. Cooking, Canadian--Maritime Provinces style. 4. Cookbooks.
I. Title.

TX747.L828 2013   641.6'92   C2013-901579-5

 Canada Council for the Arts   Conseil des Arts du Canada

The publisher acknowledges the support of the Government of Canada through the Canada Book Fund of the Department of Canadian Heritage and the Canada Council for the Arts Block Grant Program.

This book is dedicated to family and friends, customers, and fellow employees who have made the first book a great success: thank you for all your support.
Hope you enjoy this book just as much.

CONTENTS

STOCKS

STOCKS

Stocks are a good place to begin, as most sauces, stocks, soups, and other things you continually do in the kitchen start with a good stock. When making stock, you have to think about your end product. There's no sense in wasting time producing a fine dice of vegetables only to purée it. And when it comes to stocks, size *does* matter. For instance, the bigger the bones, the longer it takes to release the nutrients and flavours that you are looking for; thus the vegetables you use should be the appropriate size for the cooking time needed. For example, beef bones need a very large, coarse chop (meaning large-chop vegetables), and chicken or fish bones will need a finer cut (meaning smaller-chop vegetables). Going against tradition, I don't normally season stocks: I leave this until the very last product – no sense in seasoning twice. This makes more sense when you think of reducing a stock. When reducing, you are intensifying flavours, so you don't really want to increase the taste of salt in that process. Remember: once it is in there, it is pretty hard to take it out.

Some people make stocks and don't even realize that they're doing it. If you think of poaching fresh shrimp, what you have just made are two things: first, a court bouillon; and, second – once you've strained it and the shrimp are removed – you have shrimp stock. Now it's up to you to decide if you're going to save the stock or throw it out. If you have a use for it, keep it. After all, why not? It will make a good base for a lot of soups, some of which you may not have thought of. This is as long as you have not overused a particular product in cooking the shrimp – onions and peppercorns being the big culprits.

Keeping things as simple as possible will allow you to have more uses for your stocks. In this section we cover beef, chicken, pork, seafood, and vegetable. You'll notice that for the most part the procedures are the same, but it is up to you to decide on what the stock is to be used for. Therefore you may want to increase or decrease a particular product. Just remember to keep notes on what you have done, making it easier to do it again next time, or to make changes to whatever it is you didn't like.

I apologize to those of you who don't have a set of scales in your kitchen. It is just easier to do this type of product by weight, as it gives a more consistent product each time you do it. And since I had to scale down these recipes to a usable volume for most home chefs, multiplying recipes by weight gives you greater accuracy in producing the same stock in a larger or smaller volume. These recipes make approximately 4 litres, so if you need 20 litres, simply multiply the recipe by 5. The process doesn't make for a good consistent product if your entire recipe is presented in cups.

Now you're thinking: where am I going to find 5 pounds of bones, and what bones should I use? The answer is simple: use what you have, what you can find, and what is available. There's no need to go buy bones from your butcher unless you absolutely need to. Again, the problem is what is suitable at home may not work in the kitchen of a restaurant and vice versa. And that goes for a lot of things. Making stocks can increase your skills in a lot of other areas. Knife skills and butchery are the first two that come to mind.

So what is a stock? At its simplest, it is the end result of boiling bones, herbs, and vegetables together and straining them. That's it – no big mystery there, now is there? Remove the bones and you have a vegetable stock or broth. And what is the difference between white and brown stock? Bake it the oven beforehand to brown the bones and vegetables. Nothing could be simpler, so let's get started.

In this section, the equipment that you need is pretty basic: a roasting pan, a brush of some type, a knife, a cutting board, a ladle for skimming, a stainless steel (see seafood stock for the reasoning behind this) stock pot large enough to hold at least 8 litres of fluid, a strainer (preferably small-mesh stainless steel) or a colander and cheesecloth, and, finally, containers for cooling stocks quickly.

Beef stock—brown and white

In a restaurant, beef bones are normally plentiful, but, at home, this may not be the case. So where do you get 5 pounds of bones? And what bones do you use? You can go to your grocery store and purchase "stew bones," but these are normally too big for making brown stock. If you get in with your local butcher, they may be able to give you what you're looking for, and it may cost you next to nothing. Otherwise, what I do it at home is build up the supply of bones stored in freezer bags in my freezer until I have enough. These are bones from steaks and roasts and ribs. Think of slow-roasting some beef ribs over large-cut vegetables. Now we have the start of a brown beef stock. Just remove the meat from ribs for sandwiches or stew or soup, and what's left is for stock. That is one way of doing it.

The bones from T-bone steaks normally have the dimensions and surface area that you are looking for, but what is lacking is connective tissue. The connective tissue is what gives your stock its body. That's why joint tissue – e.g., cartilage and knuckle joints – are best. The naturally occurring gelatine is released into the stock, giving it body. This becomes more apparent when the stock is reduced.

Remember that the bigger the bones, the bigger the vegetables – thus the longer it's going to take. For beef stock to achieve full flavour, this process can take 6 to 8 hours. But, once you bring it to a simmer, the only thing you have to do for the next 6 to 8 hours is skim it occasionally.

The next thing is to consider what vegetables you like to use. Classically it's onions, carrots, and celery, which give a very basic but flavourful stock. You can add or substitute whatever you wish, keeping in mind to avoid things that might overpower the stock. I would not use too many dark-coloured vegetables. Rather, think green and red in a stock of any kind. Mushroom caps should be avoided, although the trimmings are fine, and strong-flavoured vegetables, especially those that are strong-scented, should be avoided as well.

Seasonings for stocks should be kept basic, unless you know exactly what the stock is to be used for. Classically you're looking at parsley stems, thyme leaves and stems, bay leaves, and peppercorns – things of that nature. But if you're using stock to make Asian-inspired soup, then you may want to use Asian-inspired seasonings.

BROWN STOCK

Ingredients

5 pounds beef bones with as much connective tissue as possible
¼ cup vegetable oil*
7 litres cold water
½ pound onion, appropriate-size cut
¼ pound carrots, appropriate-size cut
¼ pound celery, appropriate-size cut
½ pound small-dice tomatoes

Optional

¼ cup red wine or brandy

If using classical seasonings consider the following: 3 or 4 bay leaves, 2 or 3 sprigs of thyme, 2 or 3 garlic cloves, some parsley stems, and black peppercorns. These can all be tied into the cheesecloth bundle (known as a sachet) and added to the stock. The seasoning is the key and is totally up to you.

*Using vegetable oil is purely up to you. This is where you can get creative and add a distinctive layer of flavour and sometimes aroma to your stock. I say to use vegetable oil mainly because sometimes the bones will not render enough oil to properly roast them without burning. If you have rendered beef fat (slowly cooked solid fat to produce a liquid fat or oil) on hand, use it instead, or perhaps add bacon drippings or ham fat to the bones. Just a thought.

Procedure

1. Preheat oven to 375° to 400°. Layer a single layer of bones in a roasting pan and toss with half the vegetable oil. Place pan in oven, turning bones occasionally to caramelize the exterior without burning. When evenly caramelized, toss bones with diced tomatoes and to coat again (tomato paste may be substituted; the procedure is the same); return to oven (until tomato product is caramelized as well). At this point, remove the contents, bones and all, and deglaze the roasting pan with the alcohol (if using) and/or water. Simply pour your liquid into the hot pan, but be careful as the alcohol will flame and the water will create steam. Use a spatula to scrape the bottom of the pan to remove the caramelized bits and add to the stock pot.

2. In a stock pot, sauté carrots, onions, and celery with other vegetables of your choice, using the remainder of the oil. Stir constantly until vegetables are well-caramelized. Add contents of roasting pan, along with deglazing liquid and the herbs you have chosen for seasoning, and top with the remaining water, adding more if necessary to completely cover contents. Be sure that nothing is stuck to the bottom of the stock pot. Bring to a boil and reduce to simmer. Do not stir, but skim occasionally to remove impurities that rise to the top. Remain at a simmering point for at least 4-6 hours to a maximum of 8 hours.

3. Strain using fine steel mesh strainer or cheesecloth-lined colander, cool as rapidly as possible, remove solidified fat from the top, and refrigerate or freeze in appropriate amounts for use later.

PROCEDURE FOR WHITE STOCK

To produce a white stock using beef bones, there are a few things you don't have to do, such as no caramelizing, no tomatoes, and everything can be done in one pot. You can use any vegetables as long as they do not have a strong-scented flavour or colour. If you are using leeks, use the white part only as you do not want anything that could discolour your stock – you want it as clear as possible. The procedure is as follows:

1. Rinse bones to remove any visible impurities; set aside.

2. Lightly sauté vegetables (think white vegetables only) in the oil of your choice. Add bones, seasoning, and water.

3. Bring to a boil; reduce to simmer.

4. Skim often – never stir – for the next 6-8 hours.

5. Strain, cool, remove solidified fat, and refrigerate or freeze in appropriate amounts.

Pork stock–brown and white

Pork stock isn't commonly used, but it is sometimes good to have some on hand when cooking leaner cuts of meat. For instance, you can use it to increase the moisture in a slow-cooking roast or to create a sauce to enhance the flavour. And it's a great way of controlling the fat in your diet without losing flavour.

You may also find that in some cooking and soup-making, pork stock is called for simply because meat may be too expensive in that country. This is a great way to extend flavour without adding extra protein.

The process for making brown pork stock is the same as for beef stock. The difference is in the flavourings. Again, keep the seasonings basic, or reflect the cooking flavours of the country of your choice.

Bones with connective tissue are often readily available. For making stocks, think of the bones from a shoulder roast, pork chops, and even ham, which are full of flavour.

BROWN STOCK

Ingredients

5 pounds pork bones
¼ cup vegetable oil* [I prefer bacon drippings or diced cap fat from a ham]
7 litres cold water
½ pound onion, appropriate-size cut
¼ pound carrots, appropriate-size cut
¼ pound celery, appropriate-size cut
½ pound small-dice tomatoes

Optional

This is where you can get creative with the seasonings. Consider what the stock will be used for and season appropriately. You may want to use red wine or brandy, or something else such as apple juice, alongside seasonings such as mustard seed. Some unusual things can also be added to the stock such as diced apples, pears, and even raisins. Remember that fruit increases the sweetness of the stock and will intensify with reductions.

¼ cup red wine or brandy
             OR
fruit juices appropriate for stock use

If using classical seasonings, consider the following: 3 or 4 bay leaves, 2 or 3 sprigs of thyme, 2 or 3 garlic cloves, some parsley stems, and black peppercorns. These can all be tied into the cheesecloth bundle (known as a sachet) and added to the stock. Seasoning to your personal preference is key.

If you think Asian, try Chinese five-spice. If using whole spices (easier to remove), you will need a combination of cinnamon, cloves, fennel seed, star anise, and perhaps Sichuan peppercorns if you can find them.

If you wish to try Caribbean, you'll need a combination of cinnamon, ginger, allspice, cloves, thyme, and, of course, hot peppers.

*Using a vegetable oil is purely up to you. If the bones you use have more than enough natural fat, no other product may be needed.

Procedure

1. Preheat oven to 375° to 400°. Layer a single layer of bones in a roasting pan and toss with half the vegetable oil. Place pan in oven, turning bones occasionally to caramelize the exterior without burning. When evenly caramelized, toss bones with diced tomatoes to coat again (tomato paste may be substituted; the procedure is the same); and return to oven until tomato product is caramelized as well. At this point, remove the contents, bones and all, and deglaze the roasting pan with half the water or your choice of flavourful liquid. Simply pour your liquid into the hot pan, but be careful as the alcohol will flame and the water will create steam. Use a spatula to scrape the bottom of the pan to remove the caramelized bits and add to the stock pot.

2. In a stockpot, sauté carrots, onions, and celery with other vegetables of your choice, using the remainder of the oil. Stir constantly until vegetables are well-caramelized. Add contents of roasting pan, along with deglazing liquid and herbs you have chosen for seasoning, and top with remainder of water, adding more if necessary to completely cover contents. Be sure that nothing is stuck to the bottom of the stock pot. Bring to a boil and reduce to simmer. Do not stir, but skim occasionally to remove impurities that rise to the top. Remain at a simmering point for at least 4-6 hours to a maximum of 8 hours.

3. Strain using a fine steel mesh strainer or cheesecloth-lined colander. Cool as rapidly as possible and refrigerate.

PROCEDURE FOR WHITE STOCK

To produce a white stock using pork bones, there are a few things you don't have to do. No caramelizing is involved, no tomatoes are used, and everything can be done in one pot. You can use any vegetables as long as they do not have a strong-scented flavour or colour. If you are using leeks, use the white part only as you do not want anything that could discolour your stock – you want it as clear as possible. The procedure is as follows:

1. Rinse bones to remove any visible impurities; set aside.

2. Lightly sauté vegetables (think white vegetables only) in the oil of your choice. Add bones, seasoning, and water.

3. Bring to a boil; reduce to simmer.

4. Skim often – never stir – for the next 6-8 hours.

5. Strain, cool, remove solidified fat, and refrigerate or freeze in appropriate amounts.

Poultry stock—brown and white

Poultry stock is one of the most useful stocks you can make. The bones are the most readily available, they are the perfect size, and they're full of the connective tissue needed for a full-body stock. And poultry bones take half the time of other stocks to produce the full flavour you're looking for. Bones include the back, neck, wings, and ankle joints. Obviously bigger birds such as turkeys will produce the 5 pounds you need from one carcass alone. Remember that when you're making poultry stock, the stronger the meat flavour of the bird, the stronger the flavour of the stock. Combining different types of poultry bones in the making of a stock isn't frowned upon, but should be done carefully. Remember that game birds will produce a gamey-tasting stock.

The next time you go to buy chicken breasts, consider buying the ones that still include the breast bone and skin. Remove the bones and the skin yourself, and place them in freezer bags in your freezer for making stock when you have time. You can do the same with chicken wings: save the wing tips. For chicken legs simply remove the two exposed joint ends at the ankle and the hip joint. Or better yet, buy whole chickens and enhance your knife skills by deboning the whole thing yourself.

Again, the procedure for making brown or white stock is exactly the same. The bones are smaller so the cooking time is less. The bones will be more plentiful, so you'll need to skim more often during the cooking process. Oil is not normally needed in this recipe as you have more than likely saved the skin and any underlying fat that was present when you deboned the birds.

Seasonings are normally the classical ones listed in the recipe, but all recipes are open for interpretation and inspiration. If you have preferred seasonings for your favourite roast chicken or turkey dinner, this is a good place to use them.

BROWN STOCK

Ingredients

5 pounds chicken or mixed poultry bones [necks, backs, wing tips, and joints]
7 litres cold water
½ pound onion, appropriate-size cut
¼ pound carrots, appropriate-size cut
¼ pound celery, appropriate-size cut
½ pound small-dice tomatoes

Optional

¼ cup white wine for deglazing

If using the classical seasonings consider the following: 3 or 4 bay leaves, 2 or 3 sprigs of thyme, 2 or 3 garlic cloves, some parsley stems, and black peppercorns. These can all be tied into the cheesecloth bundle [known as a sachet] and added to the stock. The seasoning is the key and your personal preference.

Procedure

1. Preheat oven to 375° to 400°. Layer a single layer of bones in a roasting pan. Place pan in oven, turning bones occasionally to caramelize the exterior without burning. When evenly caramelized, toss bones with diced tomatoes to coat (again, tomato paste may be substituted); the procedure is the same. Return to the oven. When caramelized, remove the contents, bones and all, reserving some of the oil found in the pan for sautéing the vegetables. Deglaze the roasting pan with the wine and/or water. Simply pour your liquid into the hot pan, but be careful as the alcohol will flame and the water will create steam. Use a spatula to scrape the bottom of the pan to remove the caramelized bits and add to the stock pot.

2. In a stockpot, sauté carrots, onions, and celery with your choice of other vegetables, using the reserved oil from the pan. Stir constantly until vegetables are well-caramelized. Add contents of roasting pan along with deglazing liquid, your choice of herbs, and top with remainder of water, adding more if necessary to completely cover contents. Ensure nothing is stuck to the bottom of the stock pot. Bring to a boil; reduce to simmer. Do not stir, but skim occasionally to remove impurities that rise to the top. Remain at a simmering point for at least 2-3 hours, to a maximum of 6 hours if using larger game bones.

3. Strain using a fine steel mesh strainer or cheesecloth-lined colander. Cool as rapidly as possible and refrigerate, remove solidified fat, and store in appropriate containers for freezing for future use.

PROCEDURE FOR WHITE STOCK

To produce a white stock using poultry bones, everything can be done in one pot. Any vegetables can be used as long as they do not have a strong-scented flavour or colour as you want it as clear as possible. For instance, if using leeks, use the white part. The procedure is as follows:

1. Rinse bones to remove any visible impurities; set aside.

2. Lightly sauté vegetables (think white vegetables only) in the oil of your choice. Add bones, seasoning, and water.

3. Bring to a boil; reduce to simmer.

4. Skim often – never stir – for at least 2-3 hours, and perhaps longer if using larger game bones.

5. Strain, cool, remove solidified fat, and refrigerate or freeze in appropriate amounts.

Shellfish stock
(lobster, crab, shrimp)

It can take a long time to build up enough shells to produce a seafood stock. Tips to remember are to buy shrimp with the shell on, and shell and devein them yourself. Save the shells in a zip lock bag in your freezer until you have enough. It takes a lot of shells to reach 5 pounds. Therefore, you may need to combine whole shrimp and reserved shells. If I was doing this I would buy them on sale.

Crab, on the other hand, may be obtained cheaply if you're in with your local fish monger. Rock or snow crab clusters normally arrive frozen at sea. They are very fragile and break quite easily; normally only full clusters are displayed. Therefore broken sections may be cheaper to buy – if not simply free for the asking. Remove the meat inside the legs and save it for other uses. Rinse the shells and use them for stock.

Lobster shells are plentiful. Wash thoroughly under cold running water to remove any tamale or roe that you may find in the body section, as these will cloud your stock and may add a very strong and undesirable aroma and flavour to the finished product.

As for shellfish, it all depends on how much shellfish you cook. The procedure for making stock from shellfish such as mussels or clams is pretty simple. They're simply steamed with a small bit of salt water and mirepoix (a dice of celery, carrots, onions) until cooked. Remove the mussels from the shells and strain out the mirepoix. The liquid remaining in the pot is then carefully strained and reserved. This is referred to as stock or liqueur – or juice as they call it in the grocery store. If you steam a lot of mussels or clams, saving the liquid might be something you do already. But, for the most part, people simply buy the liquid – canned or bottled – at their local grocery store, ensuring a clear and sand-free product.

Fish stock is always white, but sometimes when making shellfish stock with lobster or crab the shells are roasted prior to sautéing to release more of the essential oils contained in the shells. You don't need as much product, and the cooking time is significantly less. However, the one must-have thing is a stainless steel pot: I have found aluminum will leech its colour into the stock due to the natural acidity of the products used.

Ingredients

5 pounds shells
7 litres cold water
¼ cup vegetable oil
¼ pound white onion, fine-dice
⅛ pound carrot, fine-dice
  (omit if desired)
⅛ pound celery, fine-dice
⅛ pound mushroom trimmings
  (stems)

Again, the seasonings or herbs you use should reflect your end product. Or stick with the classical herbs such as bay leaves, thyme, peppercorns, and parsley (use stems only as the leaves contain too much chlorophyll and may turn your stock green). Mushroom caps may turn your stock cloudy.

Procedure

1. Be sure to use a pot big enough to hold the shells and the required amount of water. Start by sautéing your vegetables in the vegetable oil until onions are translucent.

2. Add shells and toss to coat.

3. Add the appropriate amount of water – at least enough to cover shells.

4. Add seasonings of your choice.

5. Ensure nothing is stuck to the bottom; bring to a boil; reduce to simmer.

6. Skim as needed for the next 45 minutes to an hour, depending on the thickness of the shells. Shrimp will be less (close to 30 minutes), and lobster, if hard-shell, will be approximately 45 minutes.

7. Strain using a fine stainless steel mesh strainer or cheesecloth-lined colander.

8. Transfer to containers for rapid cooling, and refrigerate as soon as possible. Remove excess solidified fat and freeze for future use in appropriate-sized containers.

Seafood (salmon, whitefish) "fumé"

It's time to do fish or to do some fumé. Fumé is simply a concentrated and reduced fish stock with white wine and lemon added. If it's reduced, it's fumé; if not, it's stock. If you make the fumé without using fish, you have made a court bouillon. Most fish stock uses white-fleshed fish, such as halibut, sole, haddock, and the like. The carcass of stronger-flavoured fish such as salmon or tuna keep the stock name of the fish carcass used.

The procedure I follow to make fish fumé is to make the stock first, then strain and reduce by half. Some procedures leave everything in the pot and reduce the stock altogether.

The carcass from a 10-pound halibut will produce 5 pounds of fillets and a frame weighing around 5 pounds which includes skin, tail, fins, and bones. Do not use the gill plate as it will make the stock cloudy, as will anything left inside the abdomen. Remember to clean the fish well.

But if you're making salmon stock, or any stock from a fish that has scales, do not use the skin. For salmon I use only the skeleton and the pin bones.

Ingredients

5 pounds fish bones or carcass, cleaned and cut to manageable-sized pieces
7 litres cold water
2 cups dry white
2 lemons juiced [save the juiced lemons to add to the stock]
¼ cup vegetable oil
¼ pound white onion, fine-dice
⅛ pound carrots, fine-dice
   [omit if desired]
⅛ pound celery, fine-dice
⅛ pound mushroom trimmings [stems]

Again, stick with the classical herbs such as bay leaves, thyme, peppercorns, and parsley stems, as these will become more pronounced when the stock is reduced.

Procedure

Use a stainless steel pot big enough to hold the carcass and the given amount of water.

1. Start by sautéing your vegetables in the vegetable oil until onions are translucent.

2. Add carcass and toss to coat. Deglaze with the lemon juice and wine.

3. Add the appropriate amount of water – at least enough to cover contents.

4. Add seasonings of your choice.

5. Ensure nothing is stuck to the bottom; bring to a boil; reduce to simmer.

6. Skim as needed for the next 30-45 minutes.

7. Strain using fine stainless steel mesh strainer or cheesecloth-lined colander.

8. Return to clean stainless steel pot; bring to a simmer and reduce by half if making fumé.

9. Transfer to containers for rapid cooling and refrigerate as soon as possible, transferring to containers if you wish to freeze it for future use.

Vegetable stock

Vegetable stock can be a catch-all, meaning anything can be used. But remember to avoid strong-scented or strong-flavoured vegetables: you don't want a vegetable stock smelling like cabbage or tasting like broccoli or turnip. In the restaurant industry this is where the previous day's salad bar product ends up. At home, it is up to you to decide what you will and will not use, as well as the quality of that product. I personally use a 1 to 1 ratio. Peppers, onions, carrots, celery, and tomatoes are all fair game for my vegetable stock. Again, the bigger the cut, the longer it will take to produce the stock.

Ingredients

½ cup vegetable oil
**½ pound each of the following
  vegetables: carrot, onion, celery,
  peppers, diced tomatoes**
7 litres water
**Traditional herbs such as bay leaves,
  peppercorns, thyme sprigs, parsley
  stems, and garlic cloves**

Procedure

1. Sauté vegetables, except for tomatoes, in a stainless steel pot large enough to hold 9 litres of water.

2. Once onions have become translucent and are beginning to caramelize, add the diced tomatoes; they should deglaze the pot.

3. Add 7 litres water; bring to a boil; reduce to a simmer.

4. Add herbs for seasoning.

5. Simmer for 30-45 minutes.

6. Using a stainless steel fine-mesh strainer, strain the stock into containers for rapid cooling and refrigeration; transfer to proper-sized containers if you wish to freeze for future use.

Clarification of stocks

The clarification of stocks is a process by which a coagulant, a corresponding ground meat, and minced vegetables, along with an acidic product, are introduced to the stock in order to remove any impurities, leaving the end product crystal clear. The end result is known as a consommé, and is considered more of a soup than a stock.

Ingredients

14 egg whites
½ cup appropriately flavoured acidic product (e.g., lemon juice, wine)
1 pound corresponding finely ground meat (beef for beef stock, chicken for chicken stock, pork for pork stock, fish for fish stock, and nothing for vegetable stock if you wish to keep it vegetarian)
1 pound fine-dice vegetables that were used in the stock
corresponding herbs that were also used

Procedure

Procedure is everything in the clarification process:

1. Whip egg whites until frothy; combine with minced meat, herbs, and acidic product.

2. Add cold, degreased stock; stir to combine.

3. Bring to a simmer, gently stirring occasionally until raft begins to form (a raft is produced when the egg whites and ground meat start to congeal and rise to the top, trapping most of the impurities in your stock on the way up).

4. When the raft reaches the top, carefully make a hole in the centre to allow the liquid to blow through. Keep in mind to make the hole big enough to get a ladle in as this is where you will be straining the liquid from once the process is complete.

5. Keep at a low simmer for at least 1 hour.

6. Using several layers of cheesecloth in a colander, strain liquid with a ladle through the hole in the raft.

7. Cool quickly and refrigerate, freezing if you wish.

Reductions and remouillage

If you find that it is expensive to make the stocks, the answer is remouillage, which means to re-wet or reuse the bones from the previously made stock. The resulting stock should use new vegetables and herbs, but the flavour and body of this second stock will be significantly less – although still usable in some instances. You will have two stocks for two different uses, but you only have to find the bones once.

All stocks can be reduced – white, brown, fish, and vegetable. Vegetable stock will not naturally have the gelatinous body of stocks made with bones, but this can be remedied with the addition of the natural gelatine product.

Procedure

If you choose to make a reduction from your stock, you will have to wait until it is completely cooled, at which point you remove any fat that has risen to the top, along with any impurities you may see. Simply pour your stock into a pot large enough to hold the amount you wish to use, and slowly simmer the stock until it has reached the point where you wish to stop, straining carefully and moving to a smaller pot as soon as possible. To make glazé, in the classical tradition, you take the amount of liquid and reduce it to one-eighth its volume, which means 1 cup is reduced to 1/8 cup, if you choose to take it that far. The resulting liquid, when cooled, resembles meat-flavoured gelatine and is able to overpower your taste buds with the intensity of your stock.

Glazé at this point is used mainly to intensify flavours in other things such as sauces and soups. It is not meant to be used by itself. But it's always nice to have some on hand.

SAUCES

SAUCES

This section of the book is given in measurements normally found in most cookbooks: cups, tablespoons, etc., as I doubt that you may need any more than perhaps a litre at a time.

When we speak of sauces, we usually mean one of the five families of sauces: either basic – which is generally referred to as main or mother sauce – or one of their derivatives. The five basic sauces are béchamel, which has milk as its base; velouté, which is based on white stock; the Espagnole family, which are sauces based on brown stocks; tomato-based sauces; and, finally, the hollandaise family, which are sauces based on eggs and butter.

All of these main or mother sauces use some type of cooked flour and butter – known as roux – as a thickener, except for some tomato-based sauces, and the hollandaise family, which uses clarified butter and egg yolk.

The classical names in today's restaurants are not normally used unless it is a true classical preparation. Mostly you'll find a better description of the sauce used to make things simpler for both the server to pronounce, and the customers to understand. An example of this would be something served with a tarragon-reduction-infused butter sauce, AKA Béarnaise sauce. You'll also find a lot of sauces which are basically the puréed fruit or vegetable and reductions of some type. Not all types of sauces will be covered in this book, but I cover a general understanding of what is involved in making the sauces.

A quick use of the Internet will allow you to discover more, but, generally speaking, taking a mother sauce and adding one or more ingredients to it gives you a derivative sauce. An example of this: béchamel sauce with sautéed onions makes sauce soubise.

The world of thickeners is just as varied as the sauces. Some are just reductions, while others use a product such as corn starch. A roux, which is equal parts flour and butter by weight, is cooked together until the desired colour is achieved, then is added to the stock. And arrowroot is another popular thickener, as are different types of flour suitable for gluten-friendly cooking.

Finally, in making sauces, this is where you will add your salt and pepper to enhance the final product.

Velouté

Here we will look at making a basic velouté using fish stock. Any white stock can be used but here we are focusing on seafood. As mentioned in the above section, you don't necessarily have to stop with this one sauce – you can make a variety of other sauces simply by adding other products to your finished velouté sauce. An example would be if you add sautéed mushrooms, some lemon juice, and some well-strained liquid from steamed mussels or clams, along with a mixture of egg yolk and cream, to your finished sauce, then reduce it and strain it, you'll have a sauce that is classically referred to as sauce Normandy. I think that gives you the idea. A little research and or imagination will lead you to others.

Ingredients

2 ounces butter (by weight, not volume)
2 ounces flour (by weight, not volume)
3 litres white fish stock, fat skimmed off and warmed
salt and white pepper to taste
  (use white pepper to maintain the white colour)

Procedure

1. In a heavy-bottomed stainless steel pot, melt the butter to combine with the flour. Since you are working with a small volume, this will happen very quickly, so make sure that your stock is warm, strained, degreased, and ready to go.

2. In a steady stream add the warm fish stock to the roux, whisking constantly to ensure no lumps result. Bring to a boil and reduce to a simmer. Cook for a minimum of 20-30 minutes, during which time your sauce will reduce slightly and thicken (20-30 minutes are necessary to remove the taste of the flour).

3. At this point, season with salt and pepper. Strain sauce to remove any lumps that may have formed. Sauce should coat the back of a spoon, have a slight fish taste, and a smooth and glossy appearance. Unfortunately, this sauce is not celiac-friendly.

4. If frozen, it may separate once thawed.

Glacé

Glazé, normally spelt with a "c," is pronounced like the word "gloss." It is a very useful sauce and quite easily made – not only from stock, but also from pan drippings from a roast, to which liquid and thickener are added. If it is a roasted protein of some type (beef or poultry), the glacé will be in the brown stock family – referred to by most people as gravy. Traditionally, glacé is a reduction, to which a little liquid of some type, along with some butter, might be whisked into the severely reduced stock just prior to serving. The final product is intense in flavour and therefore used sparingly.

At the end of the stock chapter, I explained how to make glacé, which is a reduction, plain and simple. You take 8 litres of brown or white stock, and reduce it to 1 litre by reducing it several times and moving it to a smaller and smaller pot.

Classically, to achieve sauces from the brown sauce or Espagnole family, you start with a well-cooked or brown-coloured roux to which you add same flavouring vegetables that were originally used in your stock, along with diced tomato. All of this is whisked into your warmed brown stock, and more of your same herb flavourings are then added. Cook this for about 1 hour, skimming anything that may rise to the top. The resulting sauce is referred to as brown sauce.

The next branch on the family tree is demi-glacé. This is a combination of equal parts of your original brown stock and your brown sauce. This is reduced by half again. From here all other brown sauces are made.

As you can tell by now, this family of sauces is not suitable for seafood by itself. The flavours are too harsh and overpowering for delicate seafood.

To accompany surf and turf, I like port sauce, which is simply 1 litre of the demi-glacé heated with 4 ounces of a good-quality port and a little butter whisked in. I don't generally serve the full litre at once – I guess that all depends on the size of the steak.

Basic white cream sauce (with additions and uses)

Basic white cream sauce is one of the most useful and widely used sauces at home and in the restaurant industry. It takes very little time to make, it holds well, freezes well, and can be as simple as a reduction of cream and acidic product, along with a suitable flavour or seasoning. You will find cream sauces accompanying pasta, vegetables, meats, and seafood. The thing to remember is that the sauce should complement not only what it is on, under, or mixed in with, but the entire plate. Since we're working with seafood, certain flavours come to mind. The most popular would be dill, parsley, lemon, and garlic. The one thing to remember when making cream sauces is to use a stainless steel pan so as to avoid metallic flavours and colours leaching into the cream sauce. It is most important to remember that in making reductions such as cream sauce, use the highest-quality ingredients that you can find.

Ingredients

3 tablespoons oil
3 tablespoons fresh lemon juice
4 ounces good-quality white wine
1 tablespoon minced garlic
1 shallot, minced
1 litre heavy cream
salt and pepper to taste (you may opt to use ground white pepper to keep the sauce as white as possible)

Procedure

1. Sauté shallots in stainless steel pan until opaque.

2. Deglaze with lemon juice and white wine. Whisk in cream and add garlic (adding the garlic at this stage allows for the full flavour of raw garlic to carry through the sauce).

3. Continue to whisk until the sauce is nappé (meaning that it will coat the back of a spoon and hold to both sides when you draw your finger through it).

4. Season to taste.

Note: The more delicate herbs, such as like dill, basil, and parsley, should be added to the sauce later. This is to hold the integrity of their fresh flavours. Sometimes you may want the flavour of the herbs but not see them; therefore straining is completely optional. Coarse herbs or thicker leaves may be added earlier in the process; these would be rosemary, bay leaves, or, perhaps, kaffir lime leaves. Experimentation is key – there are no rights or wrongs.

Dill Cream Sauce

Ingredients

3 tablespoons oil
3 tablespoons fresh lemon juice
4 ounces good-quality white wine
1 tablespoon minced garlic
1 shallot, minced
1 litre heavy cream
2 tablespoons fresh minced dill
salt and pepper to taste [you may opt
  to use ground white pepper to keep
  the sauce as white as possible]

Procedure

1. Sauté shallots in stainless steel pan until opaque.

2. Deglaze with lemon juice and white wine. Whisk in cream and add garlic [adding the garlic at this stage allows for the full flavour of raw garlic to carry through the sauce]

3. Continue to whisk until the sauce is nappé [meaning that it will coat the back of a spoon and hold to both sides when you draw your finger through it].

4. Add dill and season to taste.

Puréed fruit sauce (mango, pineapple) Caribbean-style

In the last number of years, fruit purée and, basically, anything sweet has made its way from the dessert table to your main course. This process can be as simple as puréeing freshly picked fruit or perhaps cooking it slightly in a simple syrup.

The resulting sauce can be plated straight out of the blender, or perhaps strained of pulp, combined with some seasonings, thickened with a starch, and slightly cooked. The resulting sauce subdues, or complements, the excessive use of salty, sour, or hot spicy food. That is where this recipe comes from. When I use a lot of hot peppers (I like them a lot) the sweetness of this sauce makes it a little more bearable for those who may not have my tolerance to the heat.

Ingredients

½ cup fresh pineapple chunks
1 whole banana
½ cup sliced mango
½ cup mango juice
⅛ cup dark rum
1 tablespoon of the following spices
   combined: allspice, cloves, ginger,
   cinnamon

Procedure

1. Purée all fruit in the blender. Add the liquids and seasoning.

2. Pour into small heavy-bottomed pot; bring to a simmer and reduce slightly (if you wish it to be thicker, add a small amount of corn starch).

3. Strain to remove all pulp.

4. Season lightly with salt and pepper, and perhaps sugar to sweeten, if desired.

Puréed vegetable sauce (roasted red pepper purée, carrot purée)

We are now at the point where we are ready to make soup. Some of the simplest soups are straight purées, usually thinned with chicken or vegetable stock. Cream is generally added before the final seasoning.

With both of these recipes, using liquid to thin and stretch out what should be a straight purée actually gives a new layer of complexity with the use of a complementary flavour. These include orange juice or ginger with the carrot sauce, or perhaps some pesto with the red pepper sauce.

To make carrot purée, simply cut peeled carrots, cover with liquid, cook until well-done, purée, strain, return to heat, reduce to desired consistency, and season.

To produce approximately 1 litre of roasted red pepper sauce, using only roasted red peppers, you would need to roast approximately 3 pounds of red peppers. In the off-season, red peppers sell for $4 per pound, so $12 is a lot to pay for 1 litre of sauce – and that's not including what your time is worth. So may I offer the following recipe to tide you over until the prices come down...

Ingredients

1 ⅓ pounds red peppers
2 cloves garlic, minced
3 tablespoons olive oil
1 tablespoon thyme
2 cups vegetable stock (or water)
1 tablespoon paprika
2 tablespoons hot sauce
1 tablespoon corn starch

Procedure

1. Combine peppers, garlic, thyme, and olive oil.

2. Char peppers over open flame on a barbecue, roast in the oven, or carefully roast over stovetop.

3. Place peppers in a bowl, cover to sweat, remove charred skin, rinse off remaining charred skin and seeds from interior, discard stem.

4. Place peppers in a pot, add vegetable stock, paprika, hot sauce, and corn starch. Using handheld blender, purée until smooth. Over medium-low heat bring to a simmer and reduce to 1 litre.

5. Season to taste with salt and pepper.

Note: Paprika and hot sauce will enhance the layers of flavour and the colour of the final product. The vegetable stock is used to increase the volume. If your vegetable stock is made with a fair quantity of peppers, the flavour will carry through; otherwise different flavour layers are produced, and the corn starch is added to thicken the final product.

SOUPS

SOUPS

Is it necessary for me to make stock if I want to make soup? No, but if you go to the supermarket and look at some labels of stocks or broth, you will be amazed at the amount of salt and other things that they put in them. I like to think of store-bought stocks as the "hot dog" of the stock world. In other words, if you have to ask what's in it, you probably don't want to use it.

Not all stocks are like that, though, as some local organic farmers are making their own or will sell you products to make your own. When you think of the time involved in making stocks, the cost is next to nothing. Again if you don't ask, you will never know.

There are different categories of soups. With clear soups, think of vegetable beef or chicken noodle. Thickened soups can be basic reductions to which cream has been added or the contents have been puréed – e.g., carrot purée and cream of mushroom. Soups that have been thickened with rice or other starches such as roux or potato are referred to as thick soups; these would include chowders and bisques. There are other classifications in the classical sense, but most soups fall under these categories.

I've scaled down these recipes to 6 to 8 servings for each recipe. Where possible I use weight instead of volume, allowing you to make the appropriate soup for 1 to 100 people just by multiplying weights.

Surf-and-turf soup

6 to 8 servings

This is one of my favourite soups. The name implies what it is: you combine steak and lobster as a soup. Once you've clarified both beef and vegetable stock, most of the work has been done. You'll need to complete several different steps before assembling this soup, including making the broth, steak, garlic crostini, Duxelle, lobster claw, and the cheese quenelle.

Broth ingredients

4 cups clarified beef broth
5 cups clarified vegetable stock
**1 6-ounce onion, sliced and cleaned
    for onion brûlée**
1 tablespoon soy sauce
1 tablespoon Worcestershire sauce
1 sprig thyme
1 garlic clove, crushed

**Optional ingredients to enhance beef flavour include 1 tablespoon steak sauce and two drops liquid smoke.

Procedure

Heat a small amount of oil in a saucepan to almost the smoking point. Add onion, sliced side down, and allow it to burn – which is called an onion brûlée. In a stock pot large enough to hold all your stock, combine ingredients, along with the onion brûlée. Bring to a boil, reduce to simmer, and hold for plating.

Steak ingredients

**1 pound small-cubed strip loin steak
    that has been cleaned of fat and
    sinew**

Procedure

Pan-sear on all sides. Cover and keep warm for plating.

Quenelle of Duxelle ingredients

5 ounces peppers, finely minced
5 ounces mushrooms, finely minced
5 ounces onion, finely minced
¼ cup vegetable oil
½ tablespoon salt
1 tablespoon pepper
2 ounces good-quality brandy

Procedure

1. In a saucepan, combine the oil with the peppers, mushrooms, and onions. Sauté until the peppers are soft and the onion is opaque. Stir in salt and pepper. When the onions start to caramelize, deglaze the pan with the brandy. Reduce heat, and allow most of the moisture to evaporate.

2. The word "quenelle" refers to the shape, which is made by taking 1 teaspoon of the Duxelle and transferring the contents to another teaspoon. Continue until you have a three-sided football-shaped mound of Duxelle. Make one per bowl and set aside for assembly.

3. For the lobster, set aside claws and/ or tails for garnishing the plate, and use the remaining meat for the cheese quenelle.

4. I use minced pieces of lobster combined with equal parts cream cheese and Boursin cheese. Combine ingredients for even distribution and soften the cheese. At this point, make the quenelle and set aside for plate assembly.

5. To make the garlic crostini, simply slice the piece of baguette on the diagonal, toast lightly, rub gently with a garlic clove, and continue to toast until completely dried out.

To plate

Divide steak evenly among bowls. Add enough broth to cover steak, place one quenelle of the Duxelle in each bowl, and top with the cheese quenelle. Garnish with crostini and some fresh herbs, and serve.

Cream of wild mushroom soup with lobster tail medallions

6 to 8 servings

This is a classic wild mushroom cream soup served atop fresh lobster tail medallions. What more could you ask for, especially in a soup?

Lobster tail medallions are simply shelled lobster tails that have been sliced thinly across the width of the tail. If you bought the tail in the shell, garnishing this soup is easy. Simply combine the tail shells with a small amount of vegetable oil. Slowly bring to a simmer, allowing the colour and flavour of the shells to leach into the oil. Strain, cool, and set aside. You have now made lobster oil, which can be drizzled around the exterior of the bowl as a garnish. Even with refrigeration, I would not use this infused oil after 3-4 days.

Soup ingredients

2 ounces dried mixed mushrooms rehydrated in hot water
8 ounces sliced button mushrooms
2 ounces minced onion
3 cloves minced garlic
¼ cup olive oil
4 cups vegetable stock
5 cups water topped up with the mushroom hydration liquid
2 bay leaves
1 tablespoon fresh thyme leaves
3 sprigs parsley, minced
3 tablespoons Dijon mustard
500 ml heavy whipping cream

Procedure

1. Rehydrate mushrooms in hot water. Once softened, strain off liquid and slice the mushrooms thinly. In a large stock pot, sauté the onions, garlic, and all the mushrooms in ¼ cup olive oil. Once the button mushrooms have softened, add vegetable stock and the full amount of water. Add the bay leaves, thyme, and parsley. Bring to a boil, reduce to a simmer, and simmer for 30 minutes covered.

2. Using an immersion blender, purée contents until smooth. Whisk in cream and Dijon mustard. Season to taste with salt and pepper. Reduce on low heat until desired consistency is achieved.

To plate

Simply pour into individual bowls, drizzle lobster oil around the exterior, sprinkle with minced fresh herbs, and garnish with lobster tail medallions.

Snow crab bisque with poached claws

6 to 8 servings

If you bought snow crab to make a crab dip, or ate snow crab last night and are left with a bunch of shells and a few claws, here's a good way to stretch it into a very filling soup suitable for any occasion. Poaching the claws isn't really necessary since around here everything is completely cooked when you buy it: just heat and serve. Garnish for the soup should be kept as simple as possible, as snow crab flavour is very light. Following the procedure for making stocks from roasted shells should make for very flavourful stock. Bisques are delicate and once the rice is added they must be stirred occasionally to prevent the rice from burning to the bottom of the pot while cooking.

Soup ingredients

5 cups crab stock, made from roasted shells
2 cups water
½ cup olive oil
2 cups whipping cream
3 ounces celery, coarsely chopped
4 ounces carrots, coarsely chopped
5 ounces red pepper, coarsely chopped
1 clove garlic, minced
2 ounces onion, minced
5 ounces rice, rinsed to remove as much starch as possible
½ cup white wine
3 bay leaves
1 sprig thyme
salt and pepper to taste
shelled crab claw and freshly minced Italian parsley and chives for garnish

Procedure

1. In a stockpot, sauté all the vegetables in the olive oil until onions are opaque. Deglaze with the wine, add stock and water, thyme and bay leaves, and bring to a boil. Reduce to a simmer, at which point add the rice, and simmer over low heat until rice is very soft and extremely overcooked but not burnt (no more than 30 minutes).

2. Remove from heat, remove bay leaf and thyme sprig, and using an immersion blender purée contents until smooth. Add cream, season to taste with salt and pepper, and reduce until desired consistency has been achieved.

To plate

Simply spoon into warmed bowls, place claws in centre of bowl, and garnish around exterior of soup with freshly minced herbs.

*Note: Seasoning with ingredients other than those mentioned is a personal preference. Try adding a little smoked Spanish paprika to enhance colour and add a little flavour.

Potato corn chowder with sautéed scallops

6 to 8 servings

This is an extremely popular soup that, depending on the size of the scallops, could also be a main dish. It is simple and straightforward and provides something for everyone, with both meat and potatoes, as well as a serving of seafood. Potatoes used for this should be of a waxy variety. If you're making a large quantity, I would suggest freezing a portion without the potatoes as they will break down in the reheating process after being frozen. For added colour I like to use a mixture of baby potatoes – redskin, yellow flesh, fingerling, and white – as well as a variety of coloured peppers. No piece should be too big to fit on a spoon.

The scallops I use are normally U-12, meaning there are fewer than 12 scallops per pound. With this size, one or two is an appetizer, and three make this a meal – especially for those big eaters. If you wish, bay scallops are completely acceptable, and save you a step as they can be added to the hot finished soup 10 minutes before serving. The larger scallops I use here are pan-seared and added after the soup has been bowled.

Ingredients

6 ounces medium diced peppers, assorted colours
3 ounces small-dice carrot
3 ounces minced onion
10 ounces corn kernels
3 ounces small-dice celery
3 cloves garlic, minced
20 ounces medium-dice mini potatoes
4 ounces cooked chopped bacon
approximately 6-8 ounces raw bacon
1 cup vegetable stock
2 cups water
2 cups whipping cream
1 tablespoon dried mixed seasoning*

* For seasoning I use a mixture of dried spices which I've put through an electric coffee mill to reduce to a fine powder. I use equal amounts of the following:

2 bay leaves
tablespoon each of celery salt, mustard seed, smoked paprika, thyme, dried minced garlic, black peppercorns, and coriander seeds
salt and pepper to taste
2 to 3 U-12 scallops per person
                OR
2 to 3 ounces bay scallops per person
¼ cup olive oil

Procedure

1. In a large stockpot, cook raw bacon until crisp. Doing this first should render enough fat to sauté the peppers, corn, carrots, onions, celery, and garlic. Add the potatoes and toss to coat.

2. Next up we add vegetable stock and enough water – approximately 2 cups – to cover the potatoes. Add the dried mixed seasoning. Bring to a boil, cover, and reduce to simmer for approximately 30 minutes, at which point check the texture of the potatoes. If they are to your liking, remove the lid and reduce the liquid to the desired consistency. Add cream, and season with salt and pepper to taste.

3. At this point you should consider if your soup is thick enough. If not, you may choose to remove a small amount of liquid and whisk in some corn starch to use as a thickener. If using this method, you should remember to whisk it separately to avoid getting any lumps, and pass the liquid through a fine mesh sieve before returning to the pot. Another option is to use other thickeners, such as a small amount of mashed potatoes, to be whisked in as an instant thickener – or perhaps potato flakes might be more to your liking. If you use potato flakes, remember the final dish contains salt and you may find the end result to be too salty.

4. Sauté your scallops over high heat if you haven't already added them to your soup. Be sure to use a large enough frying pan to hold all your scallops without crowding. Using a paper towel, lightly pat dry the scallops. Season both sides with salt and pepper. Add a small enough amount of oil to lightly coat the pan. Add scallops, and allow them to sear lightly before flipping them over.

To plate

Use warmed bowls, and portion soup into each one, trying to mound vegetables in the centre. Place desired amount of scallops on outer edge, garnish with bread sticks, and serve.

Manhattan clam chowder

6 to 8 servings

I remember someone saying to me once: "It's easy to make fresh product taste good. You just let the products speak for themselves. The trick is when all you have to use is canned and processed – making *that* taste good is a real challenge."

With that in mind, I took on the challenge of coming up with my own version of the so-called "Manhattan-style" clam chowder. Around here, soft-shelled clams are available for 3-4 months of the year, but after that – if you haven't frozen some fresh, shelled, raw clams yourself – your choices for clams are canned baby clams, or bottled chopped-up bar clams in a brine. Having that to work with I created the recipe that seems to be popular, especially with those who are having a rough morning after a long night, if you know what I mean. It's simply ended up being the mating of a Caesar with a chowder. I really didn't think of it that way until I looked at the list of ingredients.

Ingredients

4 ounces raw bacon, chopped
2 tablespoons coriander seed, toasted
4 stocks celery, medium-dice
2 carrots, medium-dice
2 ounces red onion, medium-dice
2 cloves garlic, minced
4 ounces red and green peppers, medium-dice
1 ounce vodka
1 ounce gin
1 240 ml. bottle clam juice
1 341 ml. can diced fire-roasted tomatoes
1 398 ml. can tomato juice
1 341 ml. can of clamato juice
1 cup water
½ teaspoon celery salt
½ teaspoon paprika
½ teaspoon dried mustard
2 tablespoons Worcestershire sauce
2 tablespoons hot sauce
2 tablespoons hoisin sauce
2 sprigs thyme
3 bay leaves
1 pound clams, combined [e.g., canned baby, bottle bar, fresh frozen, or preferably fresh shucked]
salt and pepper to taste

Procedure

1. In your stock pot, toast coriander seed until cracked and a golden brown. Add bacon and cook to render the fat and crisp the bacon. Sauté all vegetables until onions are opaque. Deglaze with the booze and canned tomatoes. Now add all your liquids and seasonings. Bring to a boil, reduce to simmer, and cover the pot, stirring occasionally for the next 20-30 minutes, or until your carrots are soft.

2. It's at this time that you add your clams, making sure to do it at the end so that they do not become tough.

To plate

Simply spoon into warmed bowls, mounding contents into centre. Garnish with fresh herbs and toasted home-style bread.

Lobster bisque

6 to 8 servings

A bisque of any type is confusing to some people because the bisque itself doesn't contain any lobster other than the stock made from its shells. However, garnishing lobster bisque with lobster meat is very acceptable and will normally keep the customers and guests happy. The procedure is straightforward. You need not spend a lot of time preparing vegetables, for the soup has everything puréed at the end.

The trick is making the lobster stock for the bisque as dark red as possible. The darker the red the better, as when you add the cream and purée the rice, the colour will lighten, making it more appealing to the eye.

When making the lobster stock, if possible roast shells in a small bit of oil, and use that oil and the shells to begin your stock. Ensure all your shells are clean, especially the bodies: tamale must be completely removed. Remember that adding tomato paste to the shells at the very end of roasting will impart a darker, more desirable colour to your stock.

Be sure to cool the stock and strain it several times to remove any sediment that may have formed. You could use some clarified stock, but something I would not do in the clarification process is impart some of the flavour of the meat you decide to use. And using lobster meat for clarification meat is way too expensive.

Let's assume that you've saved the oil from the roasted lobster shells that you've used to make your stock.

Ingredients

¼ cup oil, preferably lobster oil
4 ounces celery
4 ounces carrot
8 ounces red pepper
4 ounces chopped fennel
1 clove garlic, minced
2 ounces onion
5 cups lobster stock
2 cups water
2 cups cream
5 ounces rice
½ cup white wine
3 bay leaves
2 tablespoons thyme leaves
salt and pepper to taste

Optional
1 tablespoon tomato paste
2 or 3 tablespoons hot sauce
  (I like mine hot!!)

Procedure

Remember that finely cut vegetables are not necessary here as your soup is puréed at the very end. But at the same time, the finer the cut, the shorter the cooking time.

In a stockpot, sauté all your vegetables in oil until onion is opaque. Stir in rice to coat, deglaze with white wine, and add stock and water. Bring to a boil, then reduce to simmer on low for 30 minutes until rice is overcooked and all your vegetables are soft. Remove bay leaves. Purée until smooth with a handheld immersion blender; if necessary, strain to remove unwanted small chunks. Whisk in cream, and add additional stock if soup looks too thick. Season to taste with salt and pepper.

To plate

Spoon into warm bowls and garnish with your choice of some or all of the following: lobster oil, fennel sprigs, drops of hot sauce and cream, and lobster meat such as claws and/or cut lobster tail. Serve.

Gazpacho with pan-seared halibut

6 to 8 servings

Here we're taking a trip to the Mediterranean with one of my favourite soups for any time of year. If I'm in a restaurant and it's on the menu, consider it ordered. Fresh and simple and easy to make – all you need are some fresh vegetables and a blender.

Classically, this is not a soup that has a lot of seasoning to it, and that's the way I present it. Changing – or should I say adding – your own seasoning will take you to a different part of the world. Think of peppers and cilantro for Mexico, rum and tropical fruit of the Caribbean, or perhaps a curry spice for India. The choice is yours. This is one of those soups that is best served ice-cold the next day so that flavours have a chance to combine. With this in mind, I wouldn't season the soup to taste until the next day. Traditionally the soup is served with a lot of garlic croutons, but here I have used pan-fried cubed halibut fillets coated with bread crumbs that have been combined with minced parsley and garlic.

Ingredients

¼ pound tomatoes, cored, chopped, and peeled
10 ounces cucumber, peeled
3 ounces onion
3 sprigs flat leaf parsley
6 ounces sweet peppers
3 cloves garlic
3 ounces celery

Liquids are equal parts of the following, whisked together in a measuring cup. I use 2 ounces of each of vegetable stock, olive oil, fresh squeezed lemon juice, good-quality sherry or port, and beer

For halibut

3 ounces cubed halibut per person
½ cup flour for dredging
egg wash (1 egg and 1 cup of milk whisked together)
2 cups bread crumbs seasoned with fresh-minced garlic and minced flat leaf parsley
½ cup olive oil for pan-frying
salt and pepper to taste

Procedure

1. In a blender, and working in batches, purée the tomato and cucumber first, adding some of the liquid if needed. Purée until smooth. Pour liquid into stainless steel bowl and purée the remainder of the vegetables with the liquids as needed, pouring the contents of the blender into the stainless steel bowl.

2. Using a whisk, blend all your puréed batches together. Using a colander, strain off any unwanted fibre until desired consistency is achieved.

3. Cover and refrigerate for a minimum of several hours, if not an entire day, allowing the soup to rest and the flavours to marry.

4. Season to taste prior to serving and serve in chilled bowls.

To plate

When ready to serve, pan-fry the halibut cubes. Simply heat oil in skillet, coat the halibut with flour, then the egg wash, then the seasoned bread crumbs. Brown on all sides, strain off any oil on paper towels, and divide evenly among bowls as your garnish.

Red onion bisque with poached salmon and capers

6 to 8 servings

If you like lox and bagels, then this is your soup. There are a few tricks to this soup, but nothing too complicated. For your stock, you want to have the extreme onion flavour. This can be achieved by taking some regular vegetable stock and simply adding more onion. You need your stock to be a dark red colour, which you get when you use a lot of small red onions, or perhaps shallots if they are available. Include in the stock the cleaned paper-like onion skin that would normally be thrown out. The colour from the skin will leech into your stock, providing the colour you desire.

Capers can vary in size and I prefer to use the ones that you would normally find on your local grocery store shelves. These are simply pan-fried until the outer skin is a little crispy, at which point they can be set aside until ready for serving.

The salmon is poached in water and a little lemon juice. You can save the resulting liquid to be used in another soup as long as it is strained of any residue. Take the tail section of an 8-pound fish, skin it, and cut it into two pieces along where the backbone would be. You'll thus have two appropriate-sized pieces for the soup. I would normally take each of these pieces and braid them prior to poaching. This

is done by trimming the piece to an even thickness, then making four equal slices, stopping just before the end of the tail, and braiding the pieces as you would braid hair. This adds a little "wow" appeal to a somewhat ordinary soup.

Again, this soup is puréed, so don't spend a lot of time making fancy cuts with the vegetables. But remember: the smaller the cut, the less time it will take to cook.

Ingredients

¼ **cup vegetable oil**
5 ounces minced garlic
12 ounces red onion [the darker the better]
4 ounces celery
6 ounces carrots
7 ounces rice
¼ **cup white wine**
3 cups of water
5 cups vegetable stock
2 bay leaves
1 sprig thyme
1 tablespoon paprika [helps with colour]
2 cups heavy cream
salt and pepper to taste
pan-fried capers
3 ounces poached salmon per person
water and lemon juice for poaching

Procedure

1. Pan-fry capers in a small amount of vegetable oil until outer skin is slightly crisp. Remove from pan and place on paper towel until ready for service.

2. In a stockpot, heat vegetable oil and sauté vegetables until onion is slightly soft but not opaque and has not lost its colour. Add rice and toss to coat. Deglaze with white wine and add vegetable stock and water. Bring to a boil and reduce to simmer. Stir occasionally to ensure that nothing is stuck to the bottom of the pot. Cover and simmer on low heat for at least 30 minutes or until rice is overcooked and vegetables are extremely soft. Using a handheld immersion blender, purée contents until smooth, and pass contents through small-holed sieve to ensure your final product is smooth and free from clumps.

3. Return to heat and reduce to achieve desired consistency.

4. To achieve a darker colour there's no shame in adding a tablespoon or two of tomato paste. I prefer to use the roasted red pepper sauce from the previous section.

5. Whisk in cream. Season to taste with salt and pepper.

6. Poach salmon in your acidic water just prior to service.

To plate

Ladle soup into warmed bowls, place poached salmon piece against the edge, swirl in cream if desired, sprinkle with capers, and serve.

Potato leek soup with haddock

6 to 8 servings

Fish and chips anyone? That is where the inspiration comes for this. Not much else has to be said about this. It's filling and stick-to-your-ribs goodness. Just like Dad used to make when Mom wasn't around!

No, I can't say I ever had this as a kid, but I probably would have liked it as much as I do now. It's very quick and simple and, believe it or not, it can be made with some leftovers (sautéed onions, mashed potatoes, fish, and some water and milk). Who says good food has to be complicated! Just take the simple everyday food and dress it up, or dress it down, depending on your mood or the company you have.

Soup ingredients

1½ pounds potatoes, cleaned and diced
½ cup vegetable oil
10 ounces leeks, white part only
2 cloves garlic, minced
½ cup white wine
3 ounces lemon juice
2½ cups water
2½ cups milk (I like to infuse the milk with the flavour of onion, cloves, and bay leaf. I simmer all of them together briefly prior to adding the strained milk to the stockpot)
salt and pepper to taste
approximately 2½ ounces haddock loin per person; cut to resemble sticks
flour for dredging
egg wash (1 egg whisked with 1½ cups milk)

Breading ingredients*

½ cup panko bread crumbs
1½ cup potato flakes
1 tablespoon cayenne pepper
1 tablespoon ground cumin
1 tablespoon cracked pepper
1 tablespoon garlic salt
1 tablespoon dried parsley flakes

Combine the above in a bowl.

*Only use 1 cup at a time, keeping unused mixture in a sealed zip lock bag for another use.

Procedure

1. In your stock pot, heat vegetable oil and sauté garlic and leeks until the leeks are soft and transparent. Deglaze with wine and lemon juice, add potatoes, and add water and infused milk. Bring to a boil. Reduce to simmer, cover, and stir occasionally to ensure nothing is stuck to the bottom of the pot. Using a handheld immersion blender, purée contents until smooth. Reduce soup to desired consistency and season with salt and pepper.

2. In a frying pan, heat oil for pan-frying the haddock. Coat the loin pieces with flour, immerse in egg wash, coat with crumb mixture, and pan-fry until golden brown.

To plate

Simply ladle soup into warmed bowls, and garnish with fish, lemon wedge, and chopped chives.

Asian-infused salmon soup with shrimp and farkay noodles

6 to 8 servings

This is a very elegant soup. Knife skills are important in this one, as everything is "cooked" in the bowl or reheated.

The first step in making this soup is to make highly flavoured salmon stock. Once this is done, reserve 6 cups to clarify to crystal clear. In the clarification process add minced lemon grass, chopped ginger, and 2 to 3 tablespoons of Asian five spice. The resulting stock may be too strong, but it is all right to thin it down with vegetable stock. Cook the farkay noodles according to package directions, drain and rinse, and set aside for service.

The shrimp size is a personal preference. For show, I use 12-16 count shrimp that have been poached ahead of time. For convenience sake, cold-water salad shrimp work, but don't look as attractive.

Ingredients

2 ounces carrots, julienne-cut
2 ounces celery, thin diagonal-slice [think of stir-fry cut, but much thinner]
1½ ounces cooked farkay noodles per person (1 ounce dried equals three ounces cooked)
2 ounces onion, julienne-cut
6 ounces peppers (red, orange, green), deveined and julienne-cut
3-4 leaves of Napa cabbage, main stem removed, chiffonade-cut, using green parts only
2 or 3 pieces of dried lobster mushrooms, reconstituted and thinly sliced
2 or 3 pieces of dried oyster mushrooms, reconstituted and thinly sliced
3 Thai chili peppers, finely sliced shrimp [If using 12-16 count shrimp, use 1 to 3 shrimp per bowl – keep in odd numbers as even numbers are considered bad luck. If using cold-water shrimp, 1½ ounces per person is suitable.]
6 cups clarified seasoned salmon stock

Procedure

1. Poach shrimp (if necessary) and hold for service.

2. Cook, rinse, and drain farkay noodles, and hold for service.

3. Heat salmon stock to boiling, and reduce to simmer until ready for service.

4. Prepare all cut vegetables, and arrange in separate piles.

To plate

Using small bowls, take a portion of the noodles and toss them with a portion of each one of the vegetables, until well-combined. Now mound this in the centre of each bowl, and surround the mound with shrimp. Ladle hot stock over top of the mound, garnish with finely sliced Thai chili peppers, and serve.

Seafood chowder with seasoning variations

6 to 8 servings

So what do I go and do, but leave the recipe that you are looking for until the very end. The Maritimes are synonymous with chowder – with every chef and every   nothing can compete with it. I guess that's why we have chowder competitions, just to see who is the flavour of the day! All I can say is, "sorry, not interested!"

Everyone's got their own opinion, and everybody will think their recipe is the best and be very willing to tell you what exactly they don't like about the other person's recipe. I enjoy the food, and the company, but I don't get involved in the politics of chowder competitions. Realistically, a chowder is simply a potato and vegetable soup with fish and seasoning. I know I've annoyed a lot of people by saying that, so I do apologize, but here's my version of basic seafood chowder with seasoning spice variations.

Remember that vegetables should be chunky, but not so chunky that they will not fit on a spoon. When I say rough-cut seafood, I mean that you shouldn't waste time trying to get perfect cuts of fish as they will break apart with the stirring and serving of the soup. Odd-shaped fish just adds more of a homemade feel to the finished product.

Ingredients

6 ounces raw bacon, cut
5 ounces chopped celery
8 ounces chopped carrots
4 ounces chopped onion
4 ounces chopped leeks [white part only]
½ cup white wine
½ cup lemon juice
10 ounces diced potatoes
4 cups fish fumé
2 cups milk or cream
12 ounces scallops [bay scallops and/or pieces]
6 ounces shrimp [cold-water salad and/or other sizes cut to the appropriate size]
5 ounces rough-cut salmon
3 ounces rough-cut haddock
4 ounces rough-cut halibut
1 tablespoon seasoning [I use the French version; see below for ingredients]
salt and pepper to taste

Garnish

hot, freshly steamed mussels [3 per person]
large-chopped lobster meat, such as claws and/or cut tails
snow crab meat, if available
thick-cut, crusty, home-style bread

To thicken

Traditionally, a white roux is added to the pot once all the liquid is incorporated. I prefer not to use a flour and butter mixture, but rather mashed potatoes or perhaps potato flakes, leaving the seasoning with salt and pepper to the very end as both of these will probably already have salt in them.

[continued p. 56]

Procedure

In a stockpot, cook bacon to render fat and until bacon is crisp. Add vegetables, and sauté until onion is opaque. Deglaze with white wine and lemon juice. Add potatoes, then cover contents with fish fumé and milk or cream and seasoning of your choice. Do not allow it to come to a boil, but cook on low heat to bring just below the boiling point. Cover, stirring occasionally for at least 15-20 minutes or until the potatoes and carrots are ¾-cooked. At this point you can add your seafood, and stir to mix well. Shut off the heat, allowing the liquid to cook the seafood, and the residual heat to finish cooking your vegetables. Once your vegetables are cooked along with the seafood, it is time to add thickener if you choose to use a potato-based ingredient.

To plate

Serve steamed mussels separately (3 per person) to avoid getting any grit or sand in your chowder. Into warmed soup bowls ladle a portion of the chowder, mounding the contents in the centre. Remember that this is chowder, so not every bowl will have the same amount and variety of seafood in each bowl. Garnish with mussels around the outside, and lobster and snow crab (if using) on top. Add the bread and serve.

SEASONING VARIATIONS

The following is a mixture of dried herbs and spices that have been reduced to a powder form using an electric coffee mill. Having seasonings ready to use this way saves you the time and frustration of having to fish them out later on. The seasonings can be used in many other ways such as salad dressings, cream sauces, and spice rubs for meat. Here are few of my favourites.

ASIAN

Use equal parts poppy seed, sesame seed, dried orange peel, dried lemon peel, black peppercorns, star anise, fennel seed, cloves, and cinnamon.

FRENCH

6 bay leaves, lavender, chives, minced onion, celery seed, fennel seed, marjoram, cloves, orange rind, thyme, and parsley.

GREEK

Add ¼ tsp cinnamon to the following recipe if you are using 1 tablespoon of each spice: sea salt, oregano, thyme, basil, sage, rosemary, parsley, dried minced garlic, black peppercorns.

CARIBBEAN

Use equal parts allspice, cloves, nutmeg, white pepper, and ground ginger. To this add ¼ cup unsweetened shredded coconut and ¼ cup dried mango slices. To use this as a wet rub for something such as chicken, reconstitute ¼ cup of this mixture in a combination of vegetable oil, pineapple juice, and dark rum.

MAINS

Cajun shellfish gumbo

6 to 8 servings

With this dish I combine generally accepted ingredients with a not-so-generally-accepted procedure. This is another dish that can be dressed-down, depending on your budget and what your guests like. It's normally a one-pot dish, meaning everything is cooked together. I find that for a dinner party, the last thing you want is to be stuck in the kitchen trying to time this properly so your fish is not overcooked and your rice does not become paste. And it's a known fact that if you tell someone supper is at a certain time, you might be eating, at the earliest, a half-hour later. It's for those reasons that I do this in stages. Everything is cooked and ready to go, so it's just a matter of reheating and plating.

In some areas oysters would be added to this dish. I sometimes serve it with oysters, but I put them on the plate, raw on the half-shell, which adds to the presentation and gives guests the choice of having them raw or cooked. Another thing I do for presentation is reserve at least three mussels per person to be left in the shell for garnish, and, if possible, a small lobster tail – or in this case a 4-6 count shrimp to increase the "wow" factor.

I use the mixture of stocks for the gumbo normally divided equally, but that's a personal preference. I use okra as a thickener since I don't cook the rice with everything else. To avoid people being put off by the texture of the okra, I purée it. Sausage is another personal preference. For me it's chorizo; others prefer andouille. And I use the Cajun spice seasoning blend provided for the Potato corn chowder recipe mentioned previously.

Ingredients

4 cups cooked rice [I use jasmine rice which is about 1 cup raw]

6 ounces red peppers chopped large

8 ounces onions, chopped large

3 ounces celery, chopped large

6 cups stock [mix of pork, vegetable, strained liquid from mussels, water]

4 okra pods chopped

1 pound bay scallops

2 pounds mussels [reserve in the shell 3 per bowl]

1½ pounds shrimp, 16-20 count

oysters, cocktail-size, 5 per person

½ pound sausage, cut into good-sized chunks

1 ounce chopped parsley

4 green onions, sliced

1 ounce whole butter by weight for making the roux

1 ounce flour by weight for making the roux

1 tablespoon Cajun spice seasoning

3 cloves garlic

¼ pound diced Roma tomatoes

2 sprigs thyme [stems removed]

3 bay leaves

4 ounces red wine

2 ounces your favourite hot sauce

salt and pepper to season to taste

Garnish

reserved mussels, oysters, toasted garlic bread or bread of your choice (1 per serving), 1 C count poached shrimp (1 per serving)

Procedure

1. Cook the rice according to package directions. I prefer to use jasmine rice; 1 cup raw rice is more than enough for this recipe. Keep warm; hold for plating.

2. In a heavy-bottomed stock pot, melt butter; add the flour to form your roux. Cook until browned [this will happen fairly quickly]. Whisk in your mixed stock, ensuring no lumps form. Add thyme leaves, bay leaves, red wine, and hot sauce, tomatoes, garlic, and all your vegetables, and, depending on the type of sausage you choose, you may want to brown it separately before adding it to your gumbo. Andouille and chorizo sausage can be added directly. Slowly bring to a simmer and cover, stirring occasionally to check on doneness of vegetables and thickness of stock; thin as necessary.

3. In a separate pot, steam your cleaned mussels until they open. Discard any mussels that don't close prior to cooking and discard any unopened mussels after they are all cooked. Remember to reserve 3 in the shell for garnishing the finished plate, and the remainder should be shelled and set aside to be added to stock when needed. The resulting liquid in the mussel pot should be strained to remove any grit and the liquid added to your main pot.

4. Fifteen minutes prior to service is the time you want to add the 16-20 count shrimp, your scallops, and the shelled mussels.

5. Season to taste with salt and pepper.

To plate

Fluff the cooked rice with a fork, and place a mound in the centre of each warmed plate. Spoon a substantial amount of gumbo around the rice, making sure each plate has a good variety of seafood. Garnish the rice mound with your large poached shrimp. Use the space around the exterior of the plate for the reserved mussels in the shell and your shucked cocktail-size oysters. Don't forget the bread.

Paella

4 servings

Paella is a dish that is as varied as it is popular. It is named after the pan in which it is cooked – which I don't have, so I use a frying pan. This wondrous concoction normally has something for everyone. Along with root vegetables and seafood, I include chicken, sausage, and ham. One thing I must insist on is saffron for the rice.

Again, I prepare this in sections as I don't want anything to be overcooked, adding any liquids that might be rendered during the cooking process to the pot to build a symphony of flavours. Traditionalists are probably gasping for air right now: how could I tell people to cook things separately and combine them only when plating! Well, I would rather be part of the conversation with my guests than be stuck in the kitchen until we decide it is time to eat. With everything ready to go, final assembly only takes a few minutes and can easily be done as people are eating their appetizers. I find that this way works for me. Everything is done perfectly with great textures and flavours. I hope you get the same results.

FYI: This is a great starter dish for those in your group who are not big seafood-eaters.

Ingredients

2 chicken legs cut in half at the joint
2 lengths chorizo or hot Italian sausage, quartered
½ pound scallops, 20-30 count
½ pound of mussels, cleaned thoroughly
½ pound of shrimp, 16 to 20 count
¼ pound salad shrimp
¼ pound ham [optional]
6 ounces coarsely chopped carrots
3 ounces coarsely chopped peppers
3 ounces coarsely chopped onions
3 ounces coarsely chopped celery
1 cup uncooked jasmine rice
4 threads saffron, crushed
4 cups of stock [combination of chicken, tomato, vegetable, fish]
1 clove garlic, minced
2 bay leaves
2 sprigs thyme
salt and pepper to taste

Procedure

1. Since the stock is combined, it is a good way to use up all those little bits of stock left over from other uses. If you do not use all the stock in plating, the remainder is a good start for bouillabaisse stock.

2. Combine all your stocks in a large pot, and add the bay leaves, thyme, and minced garlic. Bring to a simmer, and season to taste with salt and pepper.

3. Cook the rice according to package directions, adding the crushed saffron threads. Cover and keep warm for plating.

4. Season the chicken with salt and pepper and brown in a pan. Cook it in the oven at 350°, adding any rendered juices to your stock. This is done to ensure a crisp skin on the chicken. Reduce oven heat to 200°, to keep warm and ready for plating.

5. In a very large frying pan, brown your sausage and finish cooking. Add vegetables and ham, and cover contents with the combined stock. Bring to a low simmer, cover, and cook until carrots are tender.

6. Fifteen minutes before serving, add scallops and all your shrimp. Stir to combine. Add mussels at the very end, cover your pan, and increase your heat slightly. When the mussels are open you are ready to serve.

To plate

One option here is to use a large platter. Place the rice in the centre, and arrange the contents of your pan around the outside, garnishing with the roasted chicken and mussels. Place a small amount of the liquid onto the platter, but not too much as you don't want it to spill while it's being passed around to your guests. A second option is to make a small mound of rice in the centre of each plate. Add a little liquid to form a broth on the bottom of each plate. Divide contents of the pot equally amongst bowls, garnish with the chicken and mussels, and serve.

Bouillabaisse

Serves 4

This is a French version of a fisherman's stew. It is made up of a mixture of broths that have been seasoned with herbs that are readily available. Bouillabaisse has as many variations as there are coastal fishing villages in France, each one with its own dos and don'ts in the preparation and plating of this dish. I draw on the traditional and the not-so-traditional, and on aspects of many different areas. In the stock I use tomato juice and orange juice. And as a thickener I use what is called rouille, instead of the traditional way of serving the entire dish over slices of crusty bread.

To some, eating this is confusing as they don't know what to do. Simply eat the seafood and vegetables, stirring in the rouille to the remaining broth, and finish as a soup.

Ingredients for stock

1 ½ cups fish fumé
2 ¼ cups good-quality orange juice
¼ cup tomato juice
¼ cup white wine
2 saffron threads, crushed
2 sprigs thyme
1 teaspoon peppercorns
3 parsley stems
2 bay leaves

Ingredients for rouille

1/2 cup panko bread crumbs
2 cloves garlic, minced
1 teaspoon cayenne pepper
1 teaspoon olive oil
chicken or vegetable stock
  (enough to combine)

Ingredients for bouillabaisse

1 ½ pounds mussels
¾ pound scallops, 20-30 count
¾ pound shrimp, 16-20 count
½ pound halibut, cubed
3-5 small baby potatoes per person
4 ounces each carrots, peppers,
  onions, all large-cut

To assemble rouille

It's as simple as placing bread crumbs, olive oil, minced garlic, and cayenne pepper in a bowl, mixing, and adding enough stock to form a paste. Continue mixing until smooth. Refrigerate and hold for service.

To assemble stocks

Combine all ingredients into a large pot, bring to a boil, lower to a simmer, and simmer until stock has been reduced to 4 cups. Strain and keep warm in preparation for making your stew.

To assemble bouillabaisse

Place all your vegetables in a large pot, cover with stock, bring to a simmer, cover, and cook until carrots and potatoes are fork-tender. Add shrimp, halibut, scallops, and, lastly, mussels, 15 minutes prior to service.

To plate

Divide contents equally among large bowls. Arrange mussels around the inside of the bowl and mound the vegetables in the centre. Top with a quinelle of the rouille and garnish with thyme sprigs.

Cioppino

Serves 4

I know this sounds Italian, but it's actually from San Francisco. It's quick and simple: it can be a soup, but thickened with some corn starch it becomes a stew. Or, as I like to serve it with some fresh pasta, it becomes a meal in itself. Some recipes call for white wine but I like to use a full-bodied red wine such as amerona or valpolicella.

The obvious problem with cooking fish in a red wine is that your white-fleshed fish will turn red. To avoid this, you have a choice: poach the fish separately, or steam it above your dish by making a bed out of the mussels onto which you place your shrimp, then on top of that your white-fleshed fish. This requires a sauté pan with a high dome lid, or fit another pan on top to create the same idea.

Ingredients

- ½ **cup red wine**
- ¼ **cup tomatoes, skinned, seeded, and chopped**
- **1 ounce fresh basil, minced**
- **3 cloves garlic, minced**
- **2 cups fish fumé**
- **1 cup tomato juice or purée**
- **2 ounces finely chopped onion**
- **2 ounces coarsely chopped colourful peppers**
- ¼ **cup olive oil**
- **2 pounds mussels, scrubbed and cleaned very well**
- **1 pound shrimp, 16-20 count, shelled, deveined, tail on**
- **1 pound firm-flesh white fish such as halibut**

Procedure

1. In a large saucepan, heat oil, and sauté onions, peppers, and garlic. When onions are opaque, deglaze with tomatoes and/or juice, add fumé and red wine. Reduce to a simmer, add basil, stir occasionally, and season to taste with salt and pepper. When slightly reduced, add the mussels, and reduce heat slightly. When the mussels are partially open, arrange them into a single layer to form a bed. Place shrimp on top of mussels and add your whitefish on top of the shrimp. Cover with a high dome lid, and allow fish to cook thoroughly.

2. If using pasta, cook according to package directions in heavily salted water, and strain when fully cooked.

To plate

Place a small mound in the centre of the plate. Divide shrimp and white fish equally among the plates, arranging on the outer edge of the pasta. Spoon peppers and sauce around the other side of arranged fish. Lastly, divide the mussels up among the plates, placing them at evenly spaced intervals. Garnish with crusty bread sticks and coarsely chopped parsley.

Lobster risotto

Serves 4

One of my favourites dishes – when prepared properly, nothing beats this. The making of risotto varies from restaurant to restaurant. Some place everything in a pot and just let it cook, while others take a more traditional approach, ladling hot liquid into the rice and stirring gently but constantly until absorbed and then adding more hot liquid and repeating the process until the risotto is cooked. If this sounds time-consuming, it is.

This is a good way to make two 1-pound lobsters feed four people. You use the shells to make the stock, and the meat to garnish the risotto. There is nothing wrong with adding vegetables to this dish, but keep in mind that they may render liquids into your rice and discolour it. So I opt for salad on the side.

If this is your first attempt at making risotto, don't be afraid. As long as your rice is not overcooked, the liquid can be thinned down. Properly made risotto, when spooned into a mound, should hold its shape briefly when flown back into the bowl. Liquid around the outer side of the plate should be a consistency somewhere between water and cream. You should be able to see individual grains of the rice itself, and when they are bitten they have some resistance in the chewing, as well as a little bit of crunch.

I like to add the lobster meat at the very end, or use it as a garnish. This way you ensure that it is not overcooked, and the meat adds just that right amount of moisture to the dish.

This can be an expensive dish to prepare, but well worth it if done properly.

Ingredients

2 1-pound lobsters, cooked, shelled, and meat coarsely chopped
            OR
1 pound cooked lobster meat, separated and coarsely chopped, reserving the claws for garnish
¼ cup olive oil
2 ounces finely minced shallots
1 clove garlic, finely minced
3 sprigs thyme, stems removed
2 bay leaves
2 cups Arborio rice
4 cups lobster stock, hot
2 ounces lemon juice
4 ounces white wine
½ cup heavy cream
½ tablespoon hot sauce

Procedure

Heat lobster stock to simmer, then set aside. In a small heavy-bottomed stock pot, heat oil and sauté shallots until translucent; add garlic and herbs. Add Arborio rice, stirring to coat. Deglaze with lemon juice and stir until absorbed. Add the white wine, stirring until it is absorbed. Ladle the hot lobster stock into rice, one scoop at a time, stirring constantly until absorbed, then add your next ladle; repeat. Continue to add stock one ladle at a time until rice is cooked or al dente. Stir in cream and hot sauce; season to taste with salt.

To plate

Gently warm your lobster meat as you plate your risotto. On warmed plates, scoop a portion onto the centre of each plate, allowing it to flow to the edges. Remember that there should be some liquid to the outer edges of the plate. Garnish with your warmed lobster meat and serve.

Fish stew (Caribbean-style)

Serves 4

This dish features all the Caribbean heat of a good jerk seasoning. And as with most stews it is a one-pot meal. The vegetables are coarse-cut to resemble what you would normally find in any other stew. Remember that the bigger the cut, the longer the cooking time.

Not all taste buds can handle the heat that is produced in this dish. If you use my recipe for the jerk seasoning, I would suggest adding 1 tablespoon at a time as the last thing you do before adding your fish. Also, flavours will intensify with time, so if this is made up the day before you're ready to serve it, prepare yourself for some heat.

The vegetables I use are readily available. The only one you might have trouble finding is called a Caribbean sweet potato. Instead, I use regular sweet potato which has an orange-coloured flesh and a slightly darker coloured skin. The Caribbean sweet potato has white-coloured flesh and red skin, much like a red-skinned potato. As for the seafood, use what you can find, but avoid excessively oily fish. Firm white-fleshed fish is best, and, if it is a light and flaky-fleshed fish, it is better to leave the skin on.

Ingredients

1 to 2 tablespoons store-bought jerk seasoning
>   **OR**

homemade jerk seasoning made of:
12 whole Scotch bonnet chilies, stemmed
1 large onion
8 cloves garlic
½ bunch parsley stems, cleaned really well
½ bunch cilantro roots, cleaned really well
½ inch fresh ginger, peeled
1 ½ tablespoons coarse sea salt
1 tablespoon fresh thyme
1 tablespoon allspice
1 tablespoon black pepper, crushed
½ tablespoon cinnamon
½ tablespoon nutmeg
½ tablespoon ground cloves
½ tablespoon ground cardamom
½ cup dark brown sugar
¼ cup dark rum
¼ cup orange juice

To make paste

1. Combine all liquid ingredients, whisk together and set aside.

2. Purée all other ingredients in a food processor, including the brown sugar, until almost a liquid state.

3. Slowly add whisked liquid until desired consistency is attained. You may not need all of the liquid.

[continued p. 74]

For the Stew

2 carrots
1 medium-sized sweet potato
               OR
1 medium-sized Caribbean sweet
  potato
3 celery stalks
1 large Bermuda onion
3 large Roma or plum tomatoes
4 small peppers, one each red, green,
  orange, and yellow
2 cloves minced garlic
1-2 tablespoons jerk seasoning
2 cups fish stock
water as needed
2 sprigs thyme
4 stems parsley
3 bay leaves
1 pound shrimp, 16-20 count,
  4 to 5 per person
¼ pound red snapper, skin on
½ pound lobster meat, coarsely
  chopped
1 pound mussels, scrubbed clean,
  4 to 5 per person
naan bread
coarsely chopped cilantro for garnish

Procedure

1. Coarsely chop your vegetables, remembering that the larger the cut, the longer cooking time [this is more important for your hard root vegetables].

2. In a large stockpot, add all your vegetables, herbs, and seasonings, covering them with the fish stock and adding enough water to cover your vegetables. Bring to a boil, cover, and reduce to a simmer. Stir occasionally for at least the next 20 minutes, or until your carrots and sweet potatoes are fork-tender.

3. At this point, remove the bay leaf, thyme sprigs, and parsley. Now I would add the jerk seasoning, 1 tablespoon at a time, until you have reached your desired heat level.

4. Five minutes before serving, add the seafood, remembering that the mussels will take longest to cook.

To plate

Plating is simply portioning out each bowl or plate. Move the lobster meat to the top so it is visible and place mussels around the exterior. Sprinkle with coarsely chopped cilantro and serve with naan bread.

Asian-style fish fondue

4 servings

Before attempting this dish, please read the recipe fully to understand how it works!

Proteins and starch products should be kept cold. Therefore, plate them in smaller quantities and replenish often.

In this recipe you'll find that the stock is a combination of stocks – usually half fish, with the other half chicken, vegetable, or pork, and sometimes even beef. The combination of stocks is seasoned with a variety of ingredients – the ones I give are suggestions only; you may or may not want to use them. The whole idea here is to experience what this dish has to offer. Traditionally, the procedure for eating this would be to eat the meat or fish first as your protein, vegetables second, followed by everybody having a bowl of pasta or rice, into which the stock – which now contains all the flavours and scents of the protein and vegetable – is spooned over it. This was the soup course. As for dessert, well, it would be simply fresh fruit of whatever variety is available.

When I do this, I make extra stock, as I find – what with evaporation and the length of time people take to enjoy it – the stock becomes extremely concentrated in flavour. The stock is the first thing to accomplish, and with it, your knife skills. Remember that you're

looking at short cooking times for your vegetables and your fish, so the size of your cuts needs to reflect that.

Larger pieces of some of the harder vegetables, such as carrots, should be partially cooked. Pasta should be ¾-cooked so that the hot stock will finish cooking the pasta. Rice should be fully cooked and can simply be reheated.

Fondue stock ingredients

2 cups fish fumé
2 cups pork stock
2 cups water
1 tablespoon whole peppercorns
1 tablespoon hoisin sauce
¼ cup white wine
3 sprigs parsley, chopped
1 carrot, chopped
1 onion, chopped
1 stock lemon grass, chopped

Vegetables

These are only suggestions, so choose your vegetables remembering that the larger cuts of root vegetables, such as carrots, should be cooked ahead of time in order to decrease the amount of time they are in your fondue pot. The rest of your vegetables should be in a julienne-style cut (for example, carrots, peppers, celery, and, perhaps, soybeans and zucchini).

Some type of cabbage should also be presented. I use Napa cabbage in two ways: shredded, or as full leaves. I cut the main part of the rib out of the full leaf, cut from an upside down "v." I then place the julienned vegetables at the lower end of the leaf, fold over the two edges to hold the vegetables in tight, and roll up the leaf from the bottom to the top to form a type of vegetable roll.

Pasta or rice

I use farkay noodles, ¾-cooked, rinsed, then spun around dessert-sized forks to form individual nests for my guests. For rice, I use jasmine, which is fully cooked according to package directions.

Procedure

1. This makes more stock than what you will need, so the remaining liquid is perfect for any Asian-inspired soup.

2. Simply bring all ingredients together to a boil, cover, and reduce to a simmer for a minimum of 30 minutes. Strain and keep warm until ready for use, at which point increase heat slightly.

Dipping sauces

These are simply combinations of the following:

soy sauce and ginger
red wine, scallions, and garlic
sweet chili sauce and lime juice
   (chili sauce recipe is the same as the Sweet chili-glazed shrimp recipe, p.80)

Seafood

I would suggest using an amount of the following, and as many different types as you can get: larger shrimp, lobster claw and knuckle, sea bass, scallops, tilapia, and red snapper. If I use a flaky delicate fish such as haddock or sole, I opt for skin-on cuts. Avoid using stronger-flavoured fish such as salmon. Do not use fish that has the skin on if it has not been scaled, as nobody likes scales floating in their food.

Specialty equipment

Smaller tapas-styled plates for individual servings, fondue forks and spoons, small-size spider (Asian cooking utensil that usually has a bamboo handle and a wire-mesh nest on the end), small-size ladle, fondue pot and burner, or tabletop adjustable butane burner and appropriate-sized stock pot.

Root vegetable stew with mussels

4 servings

This is an easy, straightforward dish. I keep the flavourings simple so that you can add your own touch. It's great on those cooler late summer nights with a large group of people, or for something different to bring a potluck supper.

Ingredients

½ **pound turnip, cubed**
1 796 ml. can diced tomatoes
½ **pound carrots, cubed**
¼ **pound parsnips, cubed**
2 cloves garlic, sliced
¾ **pound mixed baby potatoes**
1 medium-sized Spanish onion, cubed
3 bay leaves
2 sprigs thyme
2 cups chicken stock
enough fish stock to cover your
  vegetables
3 pounds mussels

**Remember that if you do not decide to cook the mussels separately you will have to thoroughly clean them to minimize the chance of grit getting into your stew. I prefer to cook them separately and strain the liquid before adding it to the stew.

Procedure

1. I prefer this stew to have more of a thin liquid stock. If you prefer thick, may I suggest that before you add the mussels you strain off as much of the liquid as you can and thicken it by whisking in 1 or 2 tablespoons of corn starch and cooking that liquid to desired consistency. Remember that when you add your mussels they will add more liquid to your stock.

2. All ingredients are added to a large stockpot – remembering that you're going to be adding 3 pounds of mussels of the top of this, so use the largest pot you have at hand. There is nothing wrong with cooking mussels separately, as I normally do, as long as the liquid is added back to your vegetable stew after being strained to remove any grit. This may help as well with the plating, as you can garnish your plates with the cooked mussels. Otherwise all vegetables are added to the stockpot and covered with your stock; add seasoning and spices. Bring contents to a boil, cover, and reduce to a simmer, cooking for approximately 20 minutes or until vegetables are fork-tender. At this point you need to decide to thicken it or not. Add mussels and cook until shells open (if you haven't cooked them separately).

Spanish lobster

4 servings

The colours abound in this dish – as do the expenses. Neither saffron-infused rice nor lobster are cheap, but the flavours are well worth it. Normally what would happen is the lobster would be partially cooked in salted boiling water, cut up, and then sautéed with your vegetables. Here I use fresh shucked lobster meat, letting someone else worry about the first part of the cooking process.

Saffron-infused rice ingredients

1 cup jasmine rice
2 threads saffron, crushed
2 tablespoons olive oil
1 clove garlic, minced
1 ounce brunoise red pepper
1 ounce brunoise green pepper
1 ⅓ cup water

Procedure

1. Heat 1 ⅓ cups water, and infuse with the saffron. When you've achieved your desired colour, add the olive oil, then the rice. Bring to a boil, cover, and remove from heat. When ready to plate, fluff with a fork, mixing in brunoise peppers.

Spanish lobster ingredients

¼ fennel bulb, thinly sliced (reserve some fronds for garnish)
2 ounces sliced red onion
2 ounces sliced green pepper
1 tablespoon capers
¼ cup sliced black olives
zest and juice of one lemon
¼ cup olive oil
1 tablespoon tomato paste
2 ounces port
1 pound freshly shucked lobster meat (keep tails and claws as whole as possible)

Procedure

1. In a large sauté pan, sauté vegetables in oil, adding capers and black olives last. Deglaze with lemon juice; stir in lobster meat. Cover and simmer under reduced heat until ready to plate. Lobster only needs to be reheated slightly, which should take no more than 5 minutes. When ready to plate, remove the lid and stir in tomato paste and port. Add salt and pepper to taste.

To plate

Mound rice into upper corner of the plate, covering remainder of plate with sautéed vegetables and sauce and topping with equal portions of lobster. Garnish with fennel fronds.

Sweet chili-glazed shrimp with ramen noodles

4 servings

The heat of this dish can be controlled by the type of dried chilli pepper used to make the glaze. It's easier to add freshly sliced hot peppers to a mild sauce than it is to try and take out or cover up the heat in a hot sauce.

As with most stir-fry dishes, the work involved is in the cutting of the vegetables and in the making of the sauce.

Ingredients for glaze

2 dried chillies, crushed as finely as possible [remember the heat factor]
3 ounces minced onion
2 tablespoons olive oil
1 clove garlic, minced
2 tablespoons brown sugar
¼ cup orange juice
1 tablespoon corn starch
salt to taste

Procedure

1. Sauté onions and garlic in oil; add crushed peppers. Mix in brown sugar and stir well until sugar is melted. Meanwhile, combine corn starch and orange juice to make a slurry, add to saucepan, stirring constantly until sauce is thickened to desired consistency. If necessary, thin it down with orange juice or rice wine vinegar to add to the acidity.

Ingredients

2 packages ramen noodles
¼ pounds 16-20 count shrimp
6 ounces (total) julienned sweet peppers in an assortment of colours
2 ounces celery, julienne-cut
2 ounces carrots, julienne-cut
¼ cup vegetable oil
1 bunch scallions, sliced diagonally
1 U-6 count shrimp per plate

Procedure

1. Cook noodles according to package instructions; rinse and keep warm, ready for plating. In a large skillet, heat oil. Start by sautéing the shrimp on one side. When shrimp is ready to be turned, add julienned peppers and vegetables. When shrimp is fully cooked, stir in 2 ounces or more of the sweet chilli sauce. This should be enough to coat the shrimp and the vegetables.

To plate

Mound a portion of the noodles in the middle of each warmed plate. Surround each mound with some of the vegetables and shrimp. Garnish each plate with freshly sliced scallions, coarsely chopped cilantro, and top off with a very large poached jumbo shrimp.

Tilapia with fettuccine and lemon basil cream sauce

4 servings

The fresh pasta with cream sauce is a good enough plate by itself. Adding tilapia to the dish just brings it to another level.

Fresh-packaged pasta is easily found in most deli sections of major supermarkets. It freezes well, but does not replace homemade. But since not many people have the time, energy, or equipment to make homemade, buying it is okay. To make portioning simpler, you may wish to purchase pasta in nests.

Ingredients

1 pound fresh fettuccine
1 medium red onion, sliced
1 medium red pepper, sliced
1 medium green pepper, sliced
½ cup olive oil
¼ cup flour
1 ½ pounds tilapia fillets, cubed or cut into manageable-sized strips
2 cups basic cream sauce [recipe p. 24]
1 bunch fresh basil leaves

Procedure

1. Cook fettuccine according to package directions in heavily salted water. Drain, rinse, and keep warm, ready for plating.

2. In a large sauté pan, heat half the oil, and sauté onions and peppers until onion is opaque. Remove from pan and divide among the warmed plates to form a base. Using the same pan, dredge fish in flour, heat second amount of oil, and brown fish on each side. Drain on paper towel and keep warm until ready to plate. As long as the pan is not too heavily crusted, you can use it to reheat your cream sauce into which you have added the basil leaves. Stir gently until sauce is nappé and leaves have slightly wilted. Season with salt and pepper to taste.

To plate

Cover the bottom of warmed plates with sautéed vegetables. In the centre of each, place a portion of pasta, topping with equal portions of tilapia. Gently spoon cream sauce over the top of each plate until a small pool forms in the base of each plate. Garnish with fresh herbs and serve immediately.